1 MONTH OF
FREE
READING

at

www.ForgottenBooks.com

By purchasing this book you are eligible for one month membership to ForgottenBooks.com, giving you unlimited access to our entire collection of over 1,000,000 titles via our web site and mobile apps.

To claim your free month visit:

www.forgottenbooks.com/free959962

ISBN 978-0-260-61937-2
PIBN 10959962

Battlefield

NINETEEN HUNDRED AND THIRTY EIGHT

JANE SINCLAIR
Editor

JUANITA CARPENTER
Business Manager

PUBLISHED ANNUALLY
BY THE STUDENT BODY OF
MARY WASHINGTON COLLEGE,
FREDERICKSBURG,
VIRGINIA

DR. EDWARD ALVEY, JUNIOR

Dedication

HE STUDENT BODY

HOLDS IT A HIGH PRIVILEGE

IN DEDICATING THE

NINETEEN THIRTY-EIGHT BATTLEFIELD

TO

DR. EDWARD ALVEY, JUNIOR

Whose ability as an instructor is acknowledged

Whose administrative efficiency is recognized

Whose gentleness of manner is unvarying

Whose fineness of poise is a steadying influence

Whose readiness to serve meets the needs of the day

Whose dealings with others is impartial and fair

Whose sunlit philosophy is both livable and lived

Whose culture is innate and beneficent

Whose friendliness is an open sesame to student life

THE BATTLEFIELD justifies its existence only to the extent it gives pleasure to those who possess it, but this year a new phase has come into its compilation— the tender grace of a day that has gone finding expression in the quaint picture of a little gentlewoman in her high frilled headdress who looks out upon you with quiet eyes that in their day delighted in the rosemary and the rue of her boxwood garden, who saw in the coat-of-arms a royal challenge, who knew self-renunciation in that farewell hour to a son, beloved, and who found strength in hours of anxiety as she lingered at the old meditation rock. And then the picture of the tomb —so quietly she sleeps under the simple shaft before which both head and heart are bowed in acknowledgment of Mary Washington.

The BATTLEFIELD holds dear the privilege of having worked with material of such nobility from out the loveliness and the courage of Colonial days in old Virginia.

CONTENTS

THE COLLEGE

This picture is thought to have been made just about the time of Mary's marriage.

The forest, primeval, through whose swaying
grace sunshine and shadow hold high carnival.

Heaven's own shifting grandeur above;
Calm, cool pines stand by.

Without the quiet growth of tree and vine,
shrub and turf; within learning importunes.

Heaven's own shifting grandeur above;
Calm, cool pines stand by.

Without the quiet growth of tree and vine,
shrub and turf; within learning importunes.

*Almost beauteous enough for the Master
of Monticello to have smiled approvingly.*

*Linger here at the matin hour to see the sun
come up like liquid glory over the tree tops.*

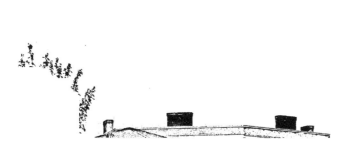

Frances Willard, the Great Ho
of those who come for the first ti
"So this is College!"

To go or to come--how eagerly the feet of
the passing pageant of girls goes treking by.

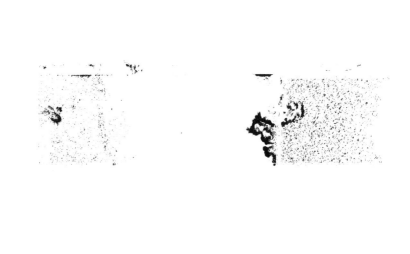

Where arch and rambling evergreen keep
tryst throughout the year.

Second only to home and comrades
fare on shoulder to shoulder.

Where one makes friends without half-
way trying and discord is an out-law.

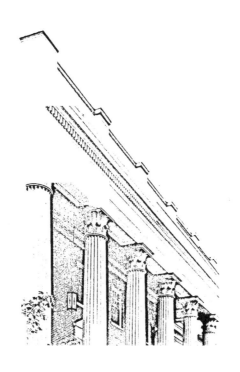

Virginia, basically collegiate, shares its roof with officialdom.

A sylvan place, this, for Roman toga or Grecian robe, for cap and gown or May Day girls or even fairies, so they say.

The bridesmaids of flower-land.

MORGAN L. COMBS
A.B., A.M., Ed.M., Ed.D.
President

A.B., University of Richmond; A.M., University of
Chicago; Ed.M. and Ed.D., Harvard University;
student, University of Berlin; travel and study in
Europe, summers 1933 and 1935. Superintendent
of Schools, Buchanan County, Virginia; State Super-
visor, Secondary Education for Virginia; Professor,
Secondary Education, Boston University; Director
Research and Surveys, Virginia State Department of
Education; Professor of Education, College of Wil-
liam and Mary, Summer School; Professor of Educa-
tion, George Washington University, Summer School.
Member, Phi Beta Kappa, Tau Kappa Alpha, Phi
Delta Kappa, and Alpha Phi Sigma. Author and
editor numerous bulletins, publications, and reports.
President, Mary Washington College,
Fredericksburg.

DR. MORGAN L. COMBS
President

The Easterns Prayer

I pray the Prayer the Easterns do: May the Peace of Allah abide with you. Wherever you stay, Wherever you go May the beautiful palms of Allah grow. Through the days of labor and nights of rest, May the Love of Sweet Allah make you blest. So I touch my heart as the Easterns do. May the Peace of Allah abide with you.

MRS. CHARLES LAKE BUSHNELL
Dean of Women

DEPARTMENT OF
COMMERCIAL
EDUCATION

Dr. James H. Dodd,
  Head of Department

Miss Lola Minich

Mr. Richard M. Kirby

Miss Ruth Rucker

Mr. Arthur L. Walker

Mr. Theodore W. Cochrane

FACULTY

DEPARTMENT OF PHYSICAL
EDUCATION

Dr. Bertha M. Kirk,
  Head of Department

Dr. Caroline B. Sinclair

Miss Sarah S. Rogers

Miss Louise E. Walraven

FACULTY

DEPARTMENT OF EDUCATION

Dr. Edward Alvey, Jr.,
    Head of Department
Mrs. James H. Dodd
Dr. Walter J. Young
Mr. E. Boyd Graves

DEPARTMENT OF SOCIAL SCIENCE

Mr. Oscar H. Darter,
    Head of Department
Mrs. R. Tipton Mooney
Dr. C. G. Gordon Moss
Dr. Almont Lindsey

FACULTY

DEPARTMENT OF ENGLISH

Dr. George E. Shankle,
Head of Department

Miss Margaret D. Calhoun,
Librarian

Miss Mary E. McKenzie
Dr. Robert F. Caverlee
Dr. Richard B. Davis
Mr. Boyce Loving
Dr. Elizabeth W. Baker

DEPARTMENT OF ART

Miss Dorothy Duggan

DEPARTMENT OF MUSIC

Miss Marion K. Chauncey
Mr. Ronald W. Faulkner
Miss Nora C. Willis

DEPARTMENT OF LANGUAGES

Miss Catesby W. Willis
Mrs. Brawner Bolling

DEPARTMENT OF SCIENCE

Dr. Roy S. Cook,
  Head of Department
Miss Helen H. Schultz
Dr. Alan S. Peirce

DEPARTMENT OF MATHEMATICS

Mr. William N. Hamlet
Dr. Hobart C. Carter

FACULTY

DEPARTMENT OF HOME ECONOMICS

Miss Mary Margaret Shaw,
  Head of Department
Miss Annabel L. Merrill
Mrs. Eula P. Robins

DIETITIAN

Mrs. John Ruff

FACULTY

ADMINISTRATION

Mr. Edgar E. Woodward, *Treasurer*
Mrs. John Ferneyhough, *Assistant Treasurer*
Miss Carolease Pollard, *Secretary to Treasurer*

Mrs. Nannie Mae M. Williams, *Registrar*
Mrs. Edmund T. Creamer, *Assistant Registrar*
Miss Katherine M. Burgess, *Secretary to President*
Dr. Edward Alvey, Jr., *Dean of the College*
Miss Dorothy A. Ramey, *Secretary to Dean*

FACULTY

DEPARTMENT OF HEALTH EDUCATION

DR. MILDRED E. SCOTT,
  Resident Physician

MISS ELIZABETH TRIBLE,
  Registered Nurse

DR. MOLLIE B. SCOTT,
  Instructor in Health Education

HOSTESSES

MRS. GORDON TAYLOR

MISS GRACE TAYLOR

MRS. HUGH BYRON MILLER

Supervisor of Freshmen and Director
of Dormitories

MISS LILLIE TURMAN

FACULTY

Mr. Charles Allmand Edwards, Principal of Training School

SUPERVISORS

Mr. Wilmer C. Berg	Miss Elinor L. Hayes	Mr. Harold H. Weiss
Miss Nena De Berry	Mr. Edward C. Stull	Miss Helen E. Mills

IN PASSING

The curtain slowly closes on a scene
That will be long remembered, though mounting years
Crowd loved memories from the heart.
Adieu, Training School!   Necessity bids you pass.
But the flames kindled within your friendly walls
Are burning in a thousand schools the world about,
And a myriad of young, free souls are glowing
With a precious fire whose spark was "College Heights."

Within these walls — the home of Mary Washington — life was lived on heights of noble ideals and sacred patriotism.

CLASSES

FRESHMAN CLASS

JEAN ROBERTSON . . . . President
NANCY MOSELEY . . . . Vice-President
BERNICE SALASKY . . . . Secretary
FRANCES GILLUM . . . . Treasurer
MR. O. H. DARTER . . . . Sponsor

FRESHMAN CLASS
HISTORY . . .

WITH shiny, new trunks full of the latest thing for the college girl, the Freshmen arrived. Their tremendous number gave some idea of the really big things they were to accomplish.

For days they were kept busy with Freshman Training—learning the things that should be done and those that should be left undone. After a few weeks this training had done them so much good that they were allowed a night of retroversion. In costume they attended the annual Kid Party to compete for the honor of being chosen the most typical child. There were all varieties of lovable juveniles at that party, including a set of Dionne Quints.

This same spirit of being young was carried on when the Athletic Association entertained the Freshmen with its annual Play Day. The new students were given the opportunity to display their athletic skill and good sportsmanship. They were given their choice of playing golf, tennis, or hockey. Horses were provided for those who preferred riding. Teams were picked at random and several rousing games ensued. With appetites whetted, the guests and their hostesses gathered about a bonfire and ate a picnic supper.

With class duties to be performed, after much serious consideration, the Freshmen elected Jean Robertson as their president. With the aid of Nancy Moseley, vice-president, she began her executive duties. Soon the Devil-Goat competition began and Bernice Salasky, secretary of the class, helped to lead the Freshmen in hunting for the Goat-hidden flag. Beneath the "Welcome" mat at Virginia Hall was too good a hiding place so the Devils had to give up the search.

The Freshmen grew up again overnight. In formal dress they attended the Student Government reception. This, too, proved an excellent opportunity to get a good look at all the Council members. In lady-like manner they filed down the receiving line and spent the evening dancing and getting acquainted.

Just a week before Christmas the Freshmen realized that peanuts were good for other things than eating. In little peanut shells, they found some student's name. Then they began to send her, anonymously, all sorts of remembrances. After a week of receiving and giving mysterious gifts, at the annual Christmas dinner, the identity of their Peanuts was made known.

With the appearance of leaves and flowers on the campus, there also began to appear on the campus little signs inviting everyone to come to the Freshman Benefit. Enticed into the gym, one found a true carnival. Startlingly, the Freshmen appeared as barkers, clowns, fortune-tellers, and jugglers. Lost in the carnival spirit and in a frenzy of spending, the patrons and the Freshmen were benefited.

At the end of May, the biggest opportunity to all Freshmen came. Work on the daisy-chain began. Over yards and yards of daisy-laden rope each Freshman was given the chance to make that chain which is a tradition in the College.

Large though it was in number and in deeds, the class has not submerged the individual. It is she who has made the Freshman Class.

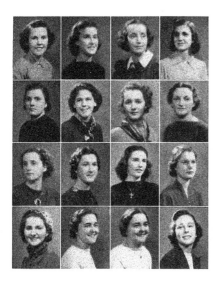

Mary Almand
Virginia Landram Alrich
Janet Alston
Ruth Annesley

Virginia Apperson
Jeanne Arnold
Anne Arnold
Lavellen Frances Ashby

Eugenia Charlotte Avery
Myrtle Bacon
Margaret Bagby
Elizabeth Bain

Vee Baker
Helen Francis Ball
Josephine Swart Ball
Addie Lee Barrett

Eleanor Batschelet·
Lorena Ann Beadles
Evelyn Beale
Frances Carolyn Bennett

Myra Birchett
Martha Black
Frances Aubrey Bolen
Dorothy Bones

Shirley Taylor Bortner
Margaret Louise Bowen
Sara Branch
Virginia Bray

Jane Carolyn Britt
Margaret Alice Britton
Juanita Brockwell
Zanie Brodie

Rose Helen Brooks
Virginia Brothers
Ellen Christine Brown
Pauline Brown

Emita Bruno
Barbara Virginia Bryant
Ruth Buchanan
Hazel Bulluck

Nancy Burch
Mildred Burner
Virginia Burnett
Emmaline Burnett

Betty Burnley
Dorothee Marie Burrman
Marion Burroughs
Helen Burrow

Betsy Burruss
Gladys Burton
Helen Burton
Maxine Calfee

Catherine Carlson
Mary Carmines
Dorothy Carney
Frances Carpenter

Virginia Creel Carpenter
Mary Carson
Elizabeth A. Carter
Elizabeth Carter

Kathryn Norma Carter
Marie Cattenhead
Roberta Anne Cecil
Mary Jane Chambers

Ann Chapman
Mary Chowning
Eugenia Clarke
Hilda Clarke

Mavis Clarke
Malcena Cleek
Virginia Dare Coates
Dorothy Cobb

Dorothy Winifred Cook
Jeanette Cooper
Elsie Mae Cornwell
Jane Cornwell

Elizabeth H. Cox
Elizabeth Cox
Mayme Lake Cox
Carol Crafton

Marjorie Creef
Mary Miller Crigler
Bennie Crist
Clara Cundiff

Elaine Daniels
Alma Darden
Dorothy Darden
Minnette Dashiell

Barber Davis
Virginia Davis
Virginia Marie Davis
Dorothy Day

Jean Lee DeCoss
Barbara Ann DePass
Ann de Vany
Isabel Herndon Dickinson

Lucy Dickinson
Norma Lee Dickinson
Alyce Dodge
Mildred Elizabeth Donaldson

Margaret Dorrier
Virginia Dougherty
Lorraine Dove
Elizabeth Mary Dowler

Beryl Duell
Marjorie Dudley
Clara Dugger
Frances Dugger

Edith Dunston
Frances Eanes
Ruth Edwards
Emma Eileen Emerson

Nancy Engleby
Virginia May Evans
Ellen Josephine Ewing
Louise Farley

Carol Faulconer
Dorothy Dunn Felts
Eloise Flanary
Juanita Fletcher

Evelyn Florence
Pauline Foster
Mildred Grace Fulton
Elizabeth Virginia Gallion

Jane Garnett
Lucille Robinson Garrett
Ruth Garrett
Mary Georgie Gay

Dorothy Marion Giles
Louise Gilland
Nancye Gillespie
Frances Gillum

Margaret Yancey Gillum
Margaret Gilman
Virginia Utah Gilmer
Annie Louise Gleason

Beatriz de Gogorza
Cordelia Goode
Raynell Goodman
Meliscent Graeff

Flora Grant
Marguerite Gregory
Virginia Grigg
Mary Virginia Gunter

Jane Reid Haddox
Betty Hall
Kathryn Harding
Betty Harker

Catherine Harris
Martha Elizabeth Harrison
Sarah Haskins
Antoinette Hayes

Miriam Maxine Hearring
Grace Hendershot
Pauline Elizabeth Hewitt
Almeda Hill

Lovey Hill
Nancy Hill
Betty Hite
Donald Claiborne Holden

Janie Elizabeth Holdren
Laura Holman
Helen Horwitz
Marie Hudson

Mary Evelyn Hudson
Bessie Conner Hull
Frances Hundley
Rebecca Hurt

Jessie Gray Hutchinson
Bernice Ison
Rhea Louise James
June Evelyn Jeffries

Martha Price Jenkins
Jane Ayers Jennings
Marguerite Jennings
Dorothy Avis Johns

Anne Johnson
Betty Jane Johnson
Marjorie Johnson
Mary Kirk Johnson

Aminee Jones
Anna Jones
Harriet Ann Jones
Marian Jones

Carol Jordan
Dena Katz
Frances Elizabeth Keister
Ella Lois Kesterson

Emeline Lois Keyser
Elizabeth Kinsman
Mildred Bonnor Kittrell
Bertha Klann

Annie Florence Land
Thelma Berniece Lane
Arabelle Laws
Caroline Lawson

Irella Lawson
Charlotte Lemley
Nancy Litton
Rosa Ellen Locke

Virginia Locke
Kathryn Lockhart
Lois Loehr
Ethel Loftin

Melba Loudy
Lida Macgill
Ruth Jeanette MacLeod
Jane McCorkindale

Myra McCormick
Betsy Anne McMath
Audrey Marcey
Jeannette Martin

Helen Maxwell
Jeanne Meads
Biddy Miller
Jane Katherine Miller

Ethel Millikin
Margaret Minter
Florence Moore
Maxine Morea

Miriam Eda Morewitz
Ruth Mosby
Jane Moseley
Julia Moseley

Nancy Moseley
Katharine Moss
Dorothy Munden
Jean Neate

Kathryn Newcome
Anne Creighton Orange
Cornelia Virginia Orr
Betty Mae Owen

Constance Owens
Phyllis Mae Pamplin
Anne Parker
Grace Meade Parker

Elaine Parks
Love Parr
Edith Patterson
Yvonne Curtis Paxson

Martha Louise Payne
Mitzi Elizabeth Payne
Doris Elinore Penn
Eleanore Royce Phillips

Nan West Phillips
Mary Lee Pittman
Rowena Powell
Marguerite Osborn Powers

Mary Frances Price
Marie Rose Pritchett
Esther James Putnam
Gayle Rainey

Charlotte Anne Ramsburg
Mildred Rawles
Wilhelmina Rawlings
Virginia Reamy

Elizabeth Reed
Mary Helen Reed
Mary Agnes Repass
Virginia Repass

Elva Reynolds
Frances Reynolds
Rosemary Rice
Margaret Roane

Beverly Roberts
Frances Roberts
Mary Frances Roberts
Jean Sager Robertson

Mary Ann Robertson
Frances Robinson
Imogene Robinson
Jane Rocap

Jeanne Rogers
Marguerite Rollins
Mary Virginia Rose
Hilda Sager

Bernice Salasky
Dorothy Sales
Grace Saunders
Alma Earle Schaeffer

Mary Ellen Seaborne
Lucy Selby
Elizabeth Carvel Shackelford
Dorothy Shaw

Kathleen Sheehan
Elizabeth Sisson
Elizabeth Cordelia Slater
Elaine Roseworth Sloope

Elizabeth Smith
Virginia Smith
Jane Raye Smith
Janet Smith

Dorothy Snead
Elizabeth May Snow
Margaret Spaven
Margaret Spivey

Louise Stawls
Polly Stephenson
Lillie Stiers
Keta Still

June Elece Stoll
Dorothy Stone
Blanche Sutherland
Rose Louise Sutton

Sara Tarr
Janet Caroline Taylor
Dorothy Thomas
Alice Thompson

Margaret Thompson
Margaret Tigner
Anne Trent
Doris Turner

Ethel Twyford
Barbara Vail
Bernice Vellines
Sara Mae Viverette

Helen Kathryn Wamsley
Elizabeth Welsh
Mary Elizabeth Werth
Ann Wheat

Jean Whitley
Mary Wyatt Whitt
Sophie Edith Wice
Anne Shirley Williams

Evelyn Williams
Frances Louise Williams
Frances Williams
Mary Williams

Nina Lee Williams
Vivian Williams
Frances Wilson
Sue Cassell Wohlford

Hester Wolffe
Rebecca Wolffe
Lorraine Wolfson
Dorothy Wood

Margery Wood
Elizabeth Woodhouse

Byrd Winston Wootton
Rena Marie Wright

Marguerite Wysor
Martha Helen Yoch

DAY AND NIGHT

Thou art ushered in
As a dew drenched morn
When Iris pulls the curtains
And Aurora brings the dawn.
Rosy fingered sunlight
Creeps upon the scene
Softly waking all the earth
Out of pleasant dreams.
Higher in the sky
Each hour the sun does rise
Smiling down on everyone
As the day goes marching by.
When evening comes at last,
Sol kisses the earth good-night
For he knows his day is past
And it is now twilight.
So again the curtain closes
On a flaming sunset
And the canopy of stars
Proclaims that it is night.

EMMA J. ZIEGLER.

SOPHOMORE CLASS

Ruth Cheshire . . . . President
Leighton Stevens . . . . Vice-President
Helen Clarke . . . . Secretary
Winifred Hudson . . . . Treasurer
Mr. Harold H. Weiss . . . . Sponsor

SOPHOMORE CLASS
HISTORY . . .

BACK to school and we were so grown-up for we were Sopho-mores, upper-classmen! The future stood before; in retrospect the past, by comparison, seemed so very young. But on our way with hopes for success . . . .

Posted announcements of class meetings heralded the fact that school routine had started again. Nominations were made for class sponsor and were referred to Dr. Combs. Our choice— Mr. Weiss.

"Blood will tell," for our sister class, the Seniors, aided us in winning the Devil-Goat contest. Together we stood! As a sisterly gesture they also willed us the privilege of upholding the precedent set by them in having for our class benefit an annual Beauty Contest.

Yes, we were superior in many ways. Didn't you hear that the Sophomore hockey team was the school champion? They de-feated the Freshmen, the Juniors, and even the Seniors. Some of our classmates rated the trip to the Hockey Tournaments at Harri-sonburg and William and Mary.

Worries began to harass our secretary, Helen Clarke, and our treasurer, Winnie Hudson, when they considered the drop in the class roll from three hundred and twenty-five to one hundred and eighty-one. You've guessed it! Class dues must be collected. One of the plans to make up for the loss in number in a financial way was the rip-roaring benefit given the last of January. Even though the Abbey Players failed to arrive, the ingenious Mr. Weiss and some of our talented classmates offered to put on a show that would equal the absent Abbeys. And that is practically what they did, for shots and screams rang out, and when the audience was not glued to the seats with fear, everyone was laughing.

Ruth Cheshire and Leighton Stevens—president and vice-president—helped us decide to entertain the Seniors with a party. With the entire class, they struggled over ideas. It must be origi-nal, for we had a reputation to uphold. It is sufficient to say that the aforementioned good name was upheld.

The oh-so-young Freshmen began struggling over the daisy chain. How vivid was our memory of the year before when, aided by our sponsor, Mr. Darter, we had toiled unto the wee hours to complete a daisy chain.

A temporary parting and its proverbial sweet sorrow are ours. There will be those of us who won't return—the missed ones. There will be those of us who will come back—the fortunate ones. Together we make our present class—the remembered ones.

Frances Marguerite Alley

Martha Selden Anderson

Ruth Rodier Anderson

Margaret E. Andrews

Margaret Adkins Austin

Mary Ann Bailey

Virginia Lee Barnes

Annie Lorraine Beck

Martha Lee Bennett

Evelyn Griffiths Berg

Florrie Mae Boldridge

Helen Louise Boothe

Rebekah Gayle Bowman

Oleta Bowman

Lula Adams Bray

Jean Beverly Broaddus

Neva Templeman Burcher

Mary Elizabeth Burnett

Carolyn Wood Carey

Margaret E. Carpenter

Fern Carson

Celia Lucille Cartwright

Mary Eloise Caverlee

Elizabeth Louise Cherry

Ruth Vivian Cheshire

Phyllis Child

Helen Holmes Clark

Ruth Francis Clark

Laura Josephine Conlon

Frances Elizabeth Cook

Sarah Elizabeth Cooke

Mary Cox

Dorothy Warren Crafton

Margaret Edmonds Cutler

Dorothy June Davis

Elsie Lee Davis

Jane Day

Dorothy Virginia DeHart

Bess Elmira Dobbins

Mildred Rebecca Dodson

Elsie Harris Dunn

Gladys Van Pelt Dutrow

Georgie Lou Easterling

Blanche Jacob Edge

Courtney Davis Edmond

Geraldine Edmondson

Sophia Eisenman

Margaret Stewart Elmore

Phyllis Knight Embrey

Mary Frances Estes

Kathryn Everhart

[55]

Aileen Louise Farmer

Virginia Lee Fiske

Alice Elizabeth Fitzhugh

Jo Lee Fleet

Elizabeth Loving Frazer

Barbara Lucille Gaines

Sylvia Garfinkel

Hubert Hilda Goode

Mary Frances Green

Mattie Rose Grizzard

Elizabeth Frances Hall

Corinna Elizabeth Hammack

Ava Clara Harrell

Hilda Naomi Harrell

Ella Laviece Harrison

Lucille Shirley Hart

Jane Constance Hawthorne

Mary Bess Hedrick

Ann Louise Hitchcock

Elsie Winifred Hudson

Rosanna Pearl Hunt

Dorothy Lucille Inscoe

Rebecca Winnie Jamerson

Rosalie Jane Johnson

Sarah DoLita Johnson

Katherine Augustus Jordan

Margaret Earle Karnes

Lee Wingate Keith

Mary Overton Kent

Virginia Alde Kilduff

Mabelle June Knopf

Evelyn Marie Lane

Evelyn Elizabeth Lasley

Juanita Bennette Lassetter

Virginia Elizabeth Lewis

Margaret Matilda Logan

Lucille Tierney Long

Dorothy Louise Luter

Jean Suzanne McCaffrey

Doris Elaine McCormic

Margaret V. McCulloch

Katrina Earle McNeal

Mary Virginia Marshall

Martha Eunice Martin

Beulah Lowe Mason

Ava Regina Matz

Mary Margaret Maxwell

Ada Eugenia Moore

Sara Vivian Moore

Charlotte Wilmath Morgan

Laura Frances Moseley

Cleo Agatha Musick

Edith Annis Neville

Virginia Lee Nichols

Mary Mitchell Noble

Margaret Anne Overman

Debra Dorothy Perlmutter

Dorothy Shepperd Persons

Charlotte Gresham Pride

Virginia Fitzgerald Ramsey

Senora Taylor Rawls

Virginia Pauline Reel

Gertrude Bain Richardson

Marjorie Dean Richardson

Katherine Lorraine Roberts

Constance Virginia Rollins

Ann Russell Rooney

Catharine Ann Rucker

Mildred Virginia Rust

Ellen Arville Sanders

Marian Johnston Schultz

Oneta Mae Shackelford

Alice Henrietta Shanklin

Nannie Louise Sharp

Rachel Davis Shelton

Mary Norvella Sledd

Ann Carolyn Smith

Cleo Gail Smith

Jane Grogan Smith

Lorraine Smith

Penelope Taylor Smith

Ellen Forrest Smoot

Sallie Elizabeth Sutton

Virginia Fann Thomas

Nan Chapman Thompson

Mary Edward Topp

Rosella Tuck

Virginia Temple Upshaw

Cecilia Grey Valentine

Eleanor Fay Wakeman

Janice Watson

Mary Louise Wilcox

Audrey Elizabeth Wood

Susan Woodward

Kathryn Wygal

Ila Dudley Yeatts

Mildred Yeatts

Mary Jane Young

Mary Lee Young

Martha Eleanor Welsh

Emma Ziegler

JUNIOR CLASS

JEANNE JOHNSON . . . . President
NAN BIRCHETT . . . . Vice-President
ARLINE GARNSEY . . . . Secretary
VIRGINIA DICKINSON . . . . Treasurer
MRS. J. H. DODD . . . . Sponsor

JUNIOR CLASS
HISTORY . . .

AFTER two years of apprenticeship the inevitable has happened—we are Juniors—with all that it stands for. The first year we were like young animals scurrying over the campus, worrying over the new and unexplainable as a naïve puppy worries over an old shoe. Nothing was left untouched by us. We learned to work this first year as we never had before. Soon another year came and we resumed our work but this time we were blasé Sophomores with a distinctly superior air. As high-and-mighty beings it was our privilege to make the benighted Freshmen jump quickly to do our bidding. "For what else were Freshmen created?" we questioned. Study again impressed its need on our wondering minds. A Minstrel Show to end all minstrel shows was presented on the stage, prepared by us, the Sophomores. This was our gift to the year of nineteen hundred and thirty-seven. Spring fever with June following it closely and the daisy chain, an old well-established custom, kept us from rushing pell-mell into all the available busses and trains bound for home. Our impulses restrained, we demure and yet defiant maidens carried the daisy chain prepared by less fortunate mortals (the Freshmen).

Juniors, the same old familiar faces with—what's this—a sprinkling of new ones and, oh, so many absent ones. Undaunted, the Class of Thirty-nine began again its trek along the royal road to knowledge.

Against a drawn blue velvet curtain there appeared a tall brown-haired girl in pink. Yes, you are right, it was Jeanne Johnson, our class president, and she announced the Junior Benefit. As a surprise to the audience, she held a colored comic sheet in her hands. Moreover, she said that it was the cast. Another surprise, our producer, director, and playwriter were one—"Bid" Bodwell. The two stepped back, the curtain parted to show a shabby room and an older woman sitting in a rocking-chair knitting. Christmas Eve and no gift for her daughter. The father entered dejectedly from a day-long tramp of the street in an unsuccessful job hunt. Fresh air and happiness were blown in with the daughter. The essential letter to Santa Claus was written asking for a doll. Again the curtains parted revealing the old familiar scene of Santa's home. Santa's two inquisitive and mischievous helpers looked after the Christmas toys. The toys were none other than the inhabitants of the "funny papers." Nothing will satisfy those elves but to wind up these mechanical toys and distribute them to various faculty members with the help of St. Nick, himself. Back to the little girl who wished so earnestly for a doll. Of course, she got it.

The party given the Freshmen by the Juniors was held in the gym on February 25th. Needless to say, it was a tremendous success.

May brought the most important social event of the year for all Juniors— the Junior-Senior Prom. Fluffy dresses and the black and white of men's dress suits add a dignity to the event.

Trusting in their past initiative and fineness and assured of a worthwhile answer, let us leave the future with a question in mind.

VIRGINIA MAE ANDERSON

MARGARET BLISS ASHBY

ELLEN MERCEREAU BAAB

NAN MASON BIRCHETT

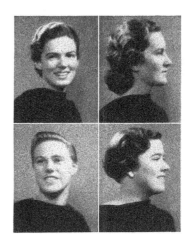

MILDRED ELIZABETH BODWELL

CHARLOTTE SCOTT BOOKER

MARY WILLIAMSON BOWLES

EULALIA BOWLING

MIRIAM REBECCA BOYER

MARY ELIZABETH BRAME

FRANCES BROOKS

VIRGINIA MAUDE BROWN

ROSEMARY BROWN

MARY ALSTON BURGESS

JUANITA SELDEN CARPENTER

MIRIAM CARPENTER

SARA ANN CHANDLER

ELIZABETH MORRIS CLOPTON

DOROTHY JANE CODDINGTON

VIRGINIA MAY COOLEY

RUTH ARCELLE COULBOURN

JANIE LEE CROWDER

RUTH PAUL CURRY

VIRGINIA THOMAS DICKINSON

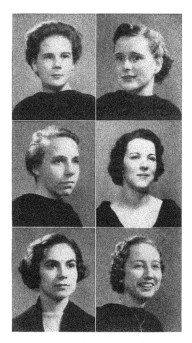

ELIZABETH DINGES

WINIFRED THERESA DOSCH

LOTTIE ELIZABETH DRIVER

MARJORIE EASTMAN

MARGARET EMERICK

ANN ETHERIDGE

[67]

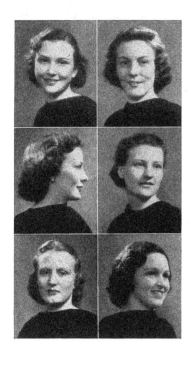

ELIZABETH YANCEY EVANS

RUTH VIRGINIA FLIPPO

MADORA FORBUSH

HAZEL BELLE FORD

HELEN FULMER

ELLA MAE FRYE

ELIZABETH WILLIAMSON GARDEN

ARLINE GAYE GARNSEY

ELEANOR GOSE

JOSEPHINE BLAIR GRAVETT

CHARLOTTE VIRGINIA HALL

LUCY OLIVER HARRIS

RUTH HARRIS

ETHEL MAE HARTMAN

ANNE TAYLOR HAZLETT

EVELYN VIRGINIA HERRING

IDA TROTMAN HILL

LAURA JEANNE JOHNSON

VIRGINIA BENNETT JONES

KATIE KEY

MARY VIRGINIA LEARY

FLORA LEE

GERALDINE McLAMB

REBA ALDA McLAMB

CONCETTA BARBARA MANGUS

LOUISE MAYES

LUCILE MILES

STELLA MILES

MABEL ETTA MOFFITT

MARY LOU MONROE

MILDRED SUE MORRIS

GERTRUDE ANN NEWNOM

BETTY LOUISE NOLAN

DORIS IRENE O'BRIEN

GILDA ORONOZ

ELNORA OVERLEY

JANET LAIRD PATTERSON

MILDRED LOUISE POWELL

GLENNIS POWERS

MARJORIE REMES

HENRIETTA ELIZABETH ROBERTS

JANE EMILIE SINCLAIR

ELEANOR SMALL

MAUDE RAE SMITH

DORIS WHITLEY STAGG

MARY CLIO STEAD

SALLY SIMPKINS STOAKLEY

JUANITA DANA STOKES

ROXIE MAXINE SUTHERLAND

NELLE THOMAS

MARION EDYTHE TIMBERLAKE

ETTA TURNER

DOROTHY CAMPBELL VERNON

LEONORA WEISS

ALYCE MILLER WENNER

EVELYN LAURA WILKINSON

MARY CLAYTON WILLIAMS

ELIZABETH WADDELL WILSON

MARGARET WOLF

GEORGIANA WOODHOUSE

BALLAD ON THE CAMPUS

Thoughts of all sizes, shapes, and worth
    Are quickly brought to mind
As I look through this BATTLEFIELD
    And familiar scenes I find.

There's Monroe—oldest, yes of all,
    Dignified and sedate,
To which I often ran in fear
    Of being, shall I say, late?

'Twas here I received assignments
    Some days reprimands too
All on account of just because
    Things I'd not done were due.

And Frances Willard—My, oh my!
    The things I'll NOT forget—
The times I was called to the window
    And brought my head in—wet!

Those nights before the holidays
    When Bedlam reigned supreme
When noise was just the thing to make
    And devilment, the theme.

Seacobeck—standing very proud
    Set off by a small brook
Where Home Ec. majors went to class
    And learned to sew and cook;

Where morning, noon, and nite we went
    To socialize and eat
Sometimes in very nice weather
    Sometimes in snow and sleet.

Virginia Hall—how often I
    Just "dropped" in to explain
Why I'd slept through the morning meal
    Or why I'd missed my train

Or asked if I could take a trip
    Or visit out of town
Or take my name off of a list
    Or stopped to put it down.

And over here, the swimming pool
    Refreshing in the fall
But in the winter, how the girls
    Would stand around and stall.

Betty Lewis, Home of the Sophs
    Just outside the gate
With 'lectric frigidaires and stoves
    These girls surely lived in state.

But give me please good Mary Ball,
    Custis or Madison
Within these walls I really learned
    The meaning of work and fun.

Social gatherings, and parties, too,
    Talks far into the night
Even after House President
    Had knocked and called "Your light!"

Now—the prettiest spot of all
    The open air theater here
Where charming maidens pay respect
    To their May Queen each year.

Beautiful in its simplicity
    Lovely in its quiet
A picture of serenity
    It's hard to pass on by it.

Faces of friends all reminders
    Of this good time and that
The girls I played some tennis with
    And those that were too fat.

The ones I liked to have around
    The ones who shared my cares
And those who lived up over me
    And those who lived down stairs

And some who I had classes with
    And some whom I did not
And some whom I remember well
    And some whom I've forgot.

It's nice to have an annual
    It helps me out a lot
In trying to remember things
    That I've almost forgot.

And if I ever grow so old
    That memories start to die,
I know 'twill serve to remind me
    Of college days gone by!

—ELIZABETH "BID" BODWELL.

SENIOR CLASS

JEAN PLANTE . . . . President
MARY JACK CLARY . . . . Vice-President
MARGUERITE CRUMLEY . . . . Secretary
SUE McGEE . . . . Treasurer
DR. C. G. GORDON MOSS . . . . Sponsor

SENIOR CLASS HISTORY

THIS Senior Class of '38 will go on record for doing the unusual. We will omit in our reminiscence those beginning days of starry-eyed bewilderment, and the two following years when we were slightly inebriated by an exalted opinion of our so-recently acquired knowledge. After laboring for some time under this delusion it dawned upon us that mayhaps the acme of erudition had not yet been reached. To avoid bestowing upon ourselves unmerited honors we will not glorify in the past, nor will we do as the gossipy bridge player who, after all the cards are on the table and the game over, tells how the hands should have been played.

Our class will be remembered for its spirit, or shall we say lack of spirit, in the Devil-Goat tradition. Conceding that the College is young, are we living up to the traditions we have? By these traditions let me tell you what the Seniors have done.

At the rally, the Devils and Goats vied in various contests. We, the Goats, emerged victorious. This victory gave us the privilege of hiding the flag. The flag was, in all probability, walked over by every student in the College, but apparently none thought of stooping to look beneath that lowly object, the doormat. By the way, who really searched? In our estimation the flag hunt was a monumental failure, not meaning thereby to condemn anyone.

The daisy chain, which we, the Seniors, consider the biggest responsibility of the Freshmen, is not just a rope of white and gold, but a revered tradition. It is the duty of each and every Freshman to dispatch this momentous task before wending homeward. Our class may be proud in this instance for its attitude, we will not say in what way unusual.

Peanut week, sponsored by the Y.W.C.A., has been our most successful tradition. This success is due no doubt to its sentiment, to the friendships started, and to the spirit of Christmas giving.

On Senior Day the full meaning of the cap and gown we wear gives us pause to ponder if by any means that tassel could be dangling from atop a cranium of vacuity. This is the day that gives us the opportunity to exhibit ostentatiously our dignified mien.

This Senior Class is known to have been the first class to select a benefit which was of such universal and lasting interest that it could be presented each year with added success. Those who attended the Beauty Contest will recall that, in the elimination process, the judges must have had a very difficult time in the presence of such a galaxy of fair women.

This Senior Class can also boast of the unique honor of having one of its members chosen not only as the school's most beautiful girl, but also chosen to reign as Queen of the May.

A social function to which Seniors unanimously look forward with avid anticipation is the Junior-Senior Prom, for this is the time when escorts are proudly paraded before envious eyes. But those unfortunate damsels, whose chosen dates find it impossible to attend, are often left with no choice but a blind date, which all too often proves fatal.

Moving-up day has at last arrived. We are alumnae and have the privileges of such. But when we think of leaving friends and familiar surroundings, we realize that the price of finishing a college education is still regret.

EVELYN ANDREWS

Major: PHYSICAL EDUCATION

DOROTHY BALLANCE

Major: COMMERCIAL EDUCATION

EVELYN BICKERS

Major: Commercial Education

IRENE BLASDEL

Major: English

VARINA BRITT

Major: COMMERCIAL EDUCATION

HELEN FORD CARTER

Major: COMMERCIAL EDUCATION

MARY JACK CLARY

Major: HOME ECONOMICS

LURA FINLEY COFFEY

Major: ENGLISH

NANCY ELOISE COOPER

Major. ENGLISH

FRANCES COX

Major: SOCIAL SCIENCE

JESSIE MARIE CROCKETT

Major: COMMERCIAL EDUCATION

MARGUERITE CRUMLEY

Major: COMMERCIAL EDUCATION

MARY LAWRENCE DAVENPORT

Major: ELEMENTARY EDUCATION

VIRGINIA JANE DAVIS

Major: HOME ECONOMICS

GLADYS PHILLIPS DICKERSON

Major: ELEMENTARY EDUCATION

VIRGINIA EASLEY

Major: PHYSICAL EDUCATION

MARGARET LOUISE GIBBENS

Major: HOME ECONOMICS

LOUISE GODWIN

Major: SCIENCE

FRANCES JO GRANT

Major: HISTORY

ANNA MAE HARRIS

Major: MATHEMATICS

MARY GRACE HAWKINS

Major: ENGLISH

MARGARET HAYNIE

Major: ELEMENTARY EDUCATION

EDNA HERSH

Major: COMMERCIAL EDUCATION

HELEN GARNETTE HILL

Major: HISTORY

CORNELIA IRBY

Major: COMMERCIAL EDUCATION

ELIZABETH JONES

Major: SOCIAL SCIENCE

[89]

VIRGINIA JORDAN

Major: HOME ECONOMICS

STIRLING KERR

Major: SOCIAL SCIENCE

MARY THERESA KETTENBECK

Major: PHYSICAL EDUCATION

VIVIAN DORIS LAFOON

Major: SCIENCE

MARY ELLEN LEE

Major: Elementary Education

MITCHELL FORREST LUCK

Major: English

IRENE LUNDY

Major: COMMERCIAL EDUCATION

MARTHA SUE McGEE

Major: COMMERCIAL EDUCATION

VIRGINIA MOORE MEEKS

Major: COMMERCIAL EDUCATION

DOROTHY MILLER

Major: SCIENCE

JEAN EVANS MOORE

Major: ENGLISH

ANNIE MAE MORRIS

Major: HOME ECONOMICS

LOUISE OTLEY

Major: COMMERCIAL EDUCATION

LUCILLE PAINTER

Major: MUSIC

LUCY PAYNE

Major: COMMERCIAL EDUCATION

KATHERINE PEARMAN

Major: HOME ECONOMICS

JEAN PLANTE

Major: COMMERCIAL EDUCATION

HELEN WADE PRESSLEY

Major: HISTORY

MARY ROBERT PUGH

Major: COMMERCIAL EDUCATION

MIRIAM MARGARET PUSTER

Major: HOME ECONOMICS

CORINNE REYNOLDS

Major: COMMERCIAL EDUCATION

ZILLAH RHOADES

Major: COMMERCIAL EDUCATION

DELLA ELIZABETH RICKS

Major: PHYSICAL EDUCATION

ALICE RIFE

Major: HOME ECONOMICS

MARY LILY RUFF

Major: COMMERCIAL EDUCATION

FLORA RYAN

Major: ELEMENTARY EDUCATION

GRACE SCHULTZ

Major: HOME ECONOMICS

BERTHA MERRILL SHAPLEIGH

Major: COMMERCIAL EDUCATION

MAY LAWRENCE SHOWARD

Major: ELEMENTARY EDUCATION

ELSIE MARIE SMITH

Major: SCIENCE

ISABEL AMELIA SMITH

Major: Mathematics

NANCY KATHERINE SNEAD

Major: English

LUCILLE SNELLINGS

Major: HOME ECONOMICS

CALVERT SPILLMAN

Major: MATHEMATICS

MARIE SPRINGER

Major: Science

CLARICE TAYLOR

Major: History

[107]

ZELMA MAE TIMBERLAKE

Major: ELEMENTARY EDUCATION

WALTEEN INEZ TOLLEY

Major: PHYSICAL EDUCATION

ELIZABETH McCLINTIC TRIMBLE

Major: HOME ECONOMICS

MARGARET TWIFORD

Major: COMMERCIAL EDUCATION

MARCELLA WELLS

Major: COMMERCIAL EDUCATION

ELIZABETH WOODBRIDGE

Major: SOCIAL SCIENCE

Hallowed places these
--the boxwood garden
onto which opens the
sun-lit dining room
of early America.

ORGANIZATIONS

LEADERS CLUB

LOUISE OTLEY . . . . President
HELEN PRESSLEY . . . . . Vice-President
JUANITA CARPENTER . . . . . Secretary
EVELYN ANDREWS . . . . . Treasurer

THE Leaders Club is an organization consisting of the leaders of departmental and social clubs, house presidents, editors of student publications, and presidents of classes and honorary sororities. It is the largest representative group of the student body and it is in this capacity that it does its best work.

The Leaders Club is the arbitrating board of all clubs. Here, in the monthly meetings, the problems of all organizations are met and solved. Here the mark of the student body is set on a smooth-running basis. The Leaders meet to present, to confer upon, and to solve the problems that slow up their particular clubs.

This year the Club undertook to sponsor the annual Red Cross Drive on the campus. It is fitting that a club composed of the leaders of the campus should carry on a drive for an organization dedicated to helping others.

THE STUDENT GOVERNMENT ASSOCIATION

FAIRNESS, loyalty to the best principles of the individual and the school, courtesy, and coöperation in all activities have been the aims of the Student Government Association since its organization.

Each member of the association, in governing herself, in setting a good example to the incoming students, and in cooperating with the college leaders and officials, plays a contributory part toward the well-being of every student.

The association functions through its representatives who constitute the Student Council. The four major officers of council, representatives from the four classes, the Day Student group, the various dormitories, and the Y.W.C.A., form a group whose interests and affiliations are widespread: The class representatives are close links between their respective classes and the organization. The house presidents of the various dormitories promote ethical standards and coöperative interest in daily campus life. The Day Student representative contributes to the organization the support and interest of those students living off the campus. The president of the Y.W.C.A., as an ex-officio member of the council, makes possible a closer bond between the two organizations.

Student Government is as effective as each member of the association makes it. Full of confidence in the student body, the organization looks forward to the time when increased individual responsibility will be the determining factor in student government.

STUDENT COUNCIL

LOUISE OTLEY . . . . President
MARY ALSTON BURGESS . . . . Vice-President
LUCY PAYNE . . . . Secretary
ELIZABETH TRIMBLE . . . . Treasurer
EVELYN ANDREWS . . House President, Mary Ball
CLARICE TAYLOR . . . House President, Madison
VIRGINIA ANDERSON . . House President, Custis
ELIZABETH WILSON . . House President, Virginia

HELEN PRESSLEY . House President, Frances Willard
MARY ROBERT PUGH . House President, Betty Lewis
CALVERT SPILLMAN . Senior Class Representative
CHARLOTTE BOOKER . Junior Class Representative
BARBARA GAINES . Sophomore Class Representative
MYRA BIRCHETT . . Freshman Class Representative
HELEN MINOR . . . Town Girl Representative
FLORA RYAN . . Ex-officio—Y.W.C.A. President

FLORA RYAN
President

YOUNG
WOMEN'S
CHRISTIAN
ASSOCIATION.

THE services of the Young Women's Christian Association at the College for this year and every year are unlimited and unforgetable—unlimited because of their every-student membership; unforgetable because of their guidance, help, and gift of pleasure to all of us.

In their efforts to raise funds for social work on the Hill and abroad, Y.W. serves breakfasts to leisure-loving students on Sunday morning and sponsors the sale of candy in the dormitories.

It is Y.W. who is in charge of the annual bonfire and Kid Party for the Freshmen. Besides this entertainment, the Cabinet, composed of six officers and fifteen committee chairmen, furnishes music for many occasions, sponsors a world fellowship for the settlement of international understanding, and better school spirit.

This year the association sent representatives to the National Assembly at Oxford, Ohio, and the annual Blue Ridge Conference at Blue Ridge, North Carolina. It has added to the education of the student body by sponsoring well-known speakers. In these and many other ways the Young Women's Christian Association had striven to fulfill the needs of a spiritual side to student life by supplementing the physical and intellectual.

Y.W.C.A. CABINET

FLORA L. RYAN . . . . . . *President*
MAUDE RAE SMITH . . . *Vice-President*
ELIZABETH WOODBRIDGE . . . *Secretary*
BERTHA SHAPLEIGH . . . . *Treasurer*
HELEN HYDE . . *Freshman Commissioner*
LOUISE OTLEY . . . . . . *Ex-officio*

CABINET MEMBERS

ELIZABETH HALL . . . . *Chairman of Social Service*
MARY ESTES . . . . *Chairman of Church Relations*
HENRIETTA ROBERTS . . . . *Chairman of Devotionals*
MILDRED POWELL . . . . . . *Chairman of Entertainment*
SARAH ANNE CHANDLER . . . . *Chairman of Finance*
MARGARET ASHBY, VIRGINIA JONES . . . . *Chairmen of Music*
MARY LOU WILCOX . . . . *Chairman of Publicity*
LUCILE MILES . . . . *Chairman of Property*
BETTY GARDEN . . . . *Chairman of Social Committee*
MADORA FORBUSH . . . . *Town Girls Representative*
JESSIE CROCKETT, KATHARINE ROBERTS . . . *Chairmen of Vespers*
MAUDE BROWN . . . . *Chairman of World Fellowship*

FACULTY ADVISORS

DR. W. J. YOUNG   MR. O. H. DARTER   DR. C. G. G. MOSS

FRESHMAN COMMISSION

OFFICERS

JEAN DeCOSS . . . . President
MARGARET GILLUM . . . . . . Vice-President
MARGUERITE JENNINGS . . . . Secretary
BETTY CARTER . . . . Treasurer
MITZIE PAYNE . . . . . Editor of Y.W. Notes

THE first leaders to be chosen by the Freshman Class are the members of the Freshman Commission. These girls serve as representatives to the Young Women's Christian Association.

No more attractive event of the current year has been presented than the Commission's annual Doll Show. Dividing the Freshmen into small groups and placing them under an upper-class leader, the Commission collected the displays made by these groups. From the many original scenes, the winners were chosen and all the shows were opened to be viewed by the student body. These dolls and the settings were sent at Christmas to the children at the Blue Ridge Sanatorium at Charlottesville, Va.

Besides their aid to all Y.W.C.A. work, the Freshman Commission members have charge of the sale of candy in the dormitories, the weekly publication of the Y.W. *Notes*, a vesper program, and a number of devotional programs.

This year's Commission has coöperated diligently with Y.W. and the Freshman Class. Its efforts in connection with the Freshman Class benefit contributed to a large extent to its success.

So drab, so bleak this project is that one wonders how slender youthful hands could have fashioned it.

THE BATTLEFIELD

EDITORIAL STAFF

JANE SINCLAIR . . . . Editor-in-Chief

MARY GRACE HAWKINS,
MARY ELLEN LEE,
MARY ALSTON BURGESS . . . . Associate Editors

MARY WILLIAMSON BOWLES . . . . Literary Editor

EMMA ZIEGLER . . . . . Assistant Literary Editor

DORIS LAFOON,
ELNORA OVERLEY,
VIRGINIA DICKINSON,
MAUDE RAE SMITH . . . . Class Editors

MARGARET ASHBY . . . . Athletic Editor

VIRGINIA ANDERSON,
ELIZABETH DINGES . . . Assistant Athletic Editors

DOROTHY BALLANCE . . . . . . Organization Editor

ROSALIE CHAUNCEY,
RUTH ANDERSON . . . . Art Editors

BUSINESS STAFF

JUANITA CARPENTER . . . . . . Business Manager

HELEN CLARK . . . . . Assistant Business Manager

ELOISE CAVERLEE . . . . . . Advertising Manager

EULALIA BOWLING,
MIRIAM CARPENTER,
FRANCES BROOKS . . Assistant Advertising Managers

NAN BIRCHETT,
ELIZABETH CLOPTON . . . . Typists

MRS. CHARLES LAKE BUSHNELL,
MISS DOROTHY DUGGAN,
DR. RICHARD DAVIS . . . . Advisers

THE BATTLEFIELD

IN this the year of our Lord, one thousand nine hundred and thirty-eight, formality and precedent is laid aside and as a group to whose lot has fallen a coveted privilege we offer a salute to the influence that comes with the name of Mary Washington. Who shall interpret a halo or who shall define an influence? Like unto a benediction, memory-laden, lavender-scented, it comes a-down the corridors of two centuries, comes so gently to the threshold of our hearts, but we shall place that influence within upon the altar, invisible, knowing it will bring uppermost whatsoever is true, whatsoever is good, whatsoever is lovely in the lives that are lived here on the heights.

THE BULLET

LED by a desire to give the members of its staff greater practical experience in the actual publishing of a newspaper, *The Bullet*, during this year, became a vastly different and more powerful force in the campus life.

Beginning in mid-winter the staff of students, under faculty guidance, began journalistic work more closely resembling that of a real up-to-date newspaper. The extensively increased staff brought with it a wider diversity of student opinions and personalities. With a united effort to attract and hold the interest of alumnae, students, and faculty, this complete representation of student thought and feeling works with deep loyalty and determination. Between each bi-weekly issue of *The Bullet* one finds the staff laboring at such tasks as proofreading, cutting and pasting the proof, and setting headlines. From this atmosphere of writing and actually making up a paper emerged a better *Bullet*. The staff wishes it to be a stepping-stone to a newspaper with the modern progressiveness which is so characteristic of the College.

THE BULLET

EDITORIAL STAFF

IRENE BLASDEL . . . . Editor

ELIZABETH BODWELL . . . . . . Associate Editor

MITCHELL FORREST LUCK,
  MARY GRACE HAWKINS,
  HELEN PRESSLEY . . . . Editorial Board

MARY LOU MONROE . . . . News Editor

MARY AGNES REPASS,
  NANCY ENGLEBY,
  MARY WELSH,
  JEAN ROBERTSON . . . . Reporters

ELOISE CAVERLEE . . . . Town News

JO LEE FLEET . . . . Feature Editor

MARGE REMES,
  ANNE ROONEY,
  MARY WELSH,
  CHARLOTTE AVERY . . . . Columnists

EMMA ZIEGLER . . . . Proof-reader

MILDRED POWELL,
  VIRGINIA DARE DOUGHERTY,
  ALMEDA HILL . . . . Make-up Editors

VIRGINIA DICKINSON,
  CORDELIA GOODE,
  ELIZABETH DAVIES,
  EUNICE MARTIN . . . . Typists

BUSINESS STAFF

DORIS O'BRIEN . . . . Business Manager

GEORGIANA WOODHOUSE . . Assistant Business Manager

ELIZABETH DINGES . . . . . . Advertising Manager

JEAN MOORE,
  LURA COFFEY,
  NITA STOKES,
  STERLING KERR,
  MADORA FORBUSH,
  CONNIE ROLLINS,
  KAY RUCKER . . . Assistant Advertising Managers

MAUDE BROWN . . . . Circulation Manager

MADORA FORBUSH,
  BERNICE WHIPPLE,
  FRANCES COOK,
  ARLINE GARNSEY,
  EVELYN BEALE,
  ELSIE LEE DAVIS,
  ANNE HAZLETT,
  CLARA HARRELL . . Assistant Circulation Managers

MR. HAROLD WEISS,
  MR. BOYCE LOVING . . . . Advisers

THE BAYONET

JÚANITA CARPENTER . . . . . *Editor-in-Chief*
EUGENIA MOORE, LUCY HARRIS . *Assistant Editors*
KATHERINE ROBERTS . . . . *Business Manager*
DR. ROY S. COOK . . . . . *Faculty Advisor*

FROM the material given to the staff by the Student Council and Y.W.C.A., *The Bayonet* organizes the rules and regulations of the College. In addition to this, the little booklet introduces the Freshmen to many phases of campus life.

The Bayonet, which is distributed to each incoming Freshman, clarifies many of the campus problems and serves particularly as a friendly guide book for them in their new surroundings.

[124]

TOWN GIRLS CLUB

ADDIBEL FREEMAN . . . . President
ELLA BLAKE . . . . Vice-President
MADORA FORBUSH . . . . Secretary
MARY BREWER . . . . . Treasurer
MR. HAROLD WEISS . . . . Sponsor

BEGINNING the first week of school, the Town Girls Club initiated its new members—those oppressed Freshmen day students. Besides the untold subservience to the wishes of upperclass day student members, they were made to dress in a most peculiar fashion. With a jolly good spirit they bore the tasks to which they were set and the stunts they were made to perform.

This initiation, however, was not all tomfoolery. By means of the things the initiates were called upon to do, the older members discovered their talents and versatility. These talents were soon put to use, as the club went about its duties, as connecting link between the girls who live on the Hill and the day students.

Never a month goes by that the Town Girls Club doesn't have a luncheon. This luncheon gives an opportunity for the discussion of problems and plans for the club. During these meetings the plans for the annual convocation program of the club are made.

When the day seems long and dull to boarding students, they are always welcome to join the fun and chatter in the attractive club-rooms of the Town Girls Club.

ALPHA PHI SI

IN true fraternal sp
ma, national hono
social and intellectu:

It is no small ho:
which requires certa
sion. Higher degree
lastic records. In :
torians and salutat:
trance to college

No initiate can :
she is entertained :
by hobby shows

The fraternity
about its convoca:
an annual custom
of one hundred :
one of the most

Gamma Chapte
from a member:
ized members

MEMBERS OF ALPHA PHI SIGMA

THIRD DEGREE: Margret Ashby, Mary Williamson Bowles, Nan Birchett, Juanita Carpenter, Phyllis Child, Mar Jack Clary, Elizabeth Clopton, Arcelle Coulbourn, Virginia Dickinson, Elsie Dunn, Betty DuPre, Sophia Eisenman, Louise Godwin, Dorothy Goodman, Anna Mae Harris, Ruth Hooker, Josephine Kislitzen, Doris Lafoon, Mary Lou Monroe, Jean Plante, Helen Pressley, Robie Pugh, Grace Schultz, Isabel Smith, Calvert Spillman, Elizabeth Trimble, Margaret Twiferd.

SECOND DEGREE: May Alston Burgess, Helen Clark, Jeanette Cooper, Dorothy Davis, Virginia Jane Davis, Gladys Dutrow, Louise Harris, Lucy Harris, Mabelle Knoff, Matilda Logan, Lucy Payne, Oneta Shacklford, Doris Stagg, Sallie Sutton, Clara Vondra, Mary Jane Young, Dorothy Ballance, Marguerit Crumley.

FIRST DEGREE: Elizabeth Alexander, Ruth Anderson, Ellen Baab, Marie Blair, Jean Broaddus, Nancy Burch, Neva Burcher, Marion Burroughs, Betsy Burruss, Mary Carmines, Eva Catafygiotu, Rosalie Chauncey, Hilda Clark, Elizabeth Cox, Mayme Lake Cox, Jessie Crockett, Murlene Crush, Jean DeCot, Isabel Dickinson, Virginia Dare Dougherty, Lottie Driver, Courtney Edmonds, Mary Este Jo Lee Fleet, Juanita Fletcher, Sylvia Garfinkel, Hilda Goode, Kathryn

ALPHA PHI SIGMA

OFFICERS

Doris Lafoon . . . . . President
Louise Godwin . . . Vice-President
Phyllis Child . . Secretary-Treasurer
Margaret Twiford,
          Statistical Secretary
Mrs. J. H. Dodd . . . . . Sponsor

IN true fraternal spirit, the Gamma Chapter of Alpha Phi Sigma, national honorary fraternity, has this year broadened in social and intellectual activity.

It is no small honor to become a member of this fraternity, which requires certain standard scholastic prerequisites for admission. Higher degrees of honor are given for continued fine scholastic records. In recognition of high school merit, all valedictorians and salutatorians are eligible for membership upon entrance to college.

No initiate can forget the original and royal manner in which she is entertained at delightful parties, followed through the year by hobby shows, and the annual banquet.

The fraternity's work of a constructive nature has centered about its convocation program and its loan fund. It has become an annual custom to present a play for convocation. The loan fund of one hundred dollars made each year to one of its members is one of the most worthwhile of the fraternity's activities.

Gamma Chapter has grown since its installation in this College from a membership of forty charter members to one of over a hundred members, eight of which are honorary.

MEMBERS OF ALPHA PHI SIGMA

THIRD DEGREE: Margaret Ashby, Mary Williamson Bowles, Nan Birchett, Juanita Carpenter, Phyllis Child, Mary Jack Clary, Elizabeth Clopton, Arcelle Coulbourn, Virginia Dickinson, Elsie Dunn, Betty DuPre, Sophia Eisenman, Louise Godwin, Dorothy Goodman, Anna Mae Harris, Ruth Hooker, Josephine Kislitzen, Doris Lafoon, Mary Lou Monroe, Jean Plante, Helen Pressley, Robbie Pugh, Grace Schultz, Isabel Smith, Calvert Spillman, Elizabeth Trimble, Margaret Twiford.

SECOND DEGREE: Mary Alston Burgess, Helen Clark, Jeanette Cooper, Dorothy Davis, Virginia Jane Davis, Gladys Dutrow, Louise Harris, Lucy Harris, Mabelle Knoff, Matilda Logan, Lucy Payne, Oneta Shackelford, Doris Stagg, Sallie Sutton, Clara Vondra, Mary Jane Young, Dorothy Ballance, Marguerite Crumley.

FIRST DEGREE: Elizabeth Alexander, Ruth Anderson, Ellen Baab, Marie Blair, Jean Broaddus, Nancy Burch, Neva Burcher, Marion Burroughs, Betsy Burruss, Mary Carmines, Eva Catafygiotu, Rosalie Chauncey, Hilda Clark, Elizabeth Cox, Mayme Lake Cox, Jessie Crockett, Murlene Crush, Jean DeCoss, Isabel Dickinson, Virginia Dare Dougherty, Lottie Driver, Courtney Edmonds, Mary Estes, Jo Lee Fleet, Juanita Fletcher, Sylvia Garfinkel, Hilda Goode, Kathryn Harding, Victoria Harris, Almeda Hill, Kathryn Jordan, Mary Ellen Lee, Eunice Martin, Eulaleur Mason, Sue McGee, Margaret Minter, Frances Mosely, Ann Orange, Lucille Painter, Mary Lee Pittman, Edith Pomeroy, Esther Putnam, Mary Agnes RePass, Marjorie Richardson, Alice Rife, Henrietta Roberts, Helen Dale Roop, Marion Schultz, Lucy Selby, Henrietta Shanklin, Bertha Shapleigh, Elizabeth Sisson, Elizabeth Snow, Margaret Spaven, Sara Mae Viverette, Janice Watson, Jean Whitley, Mary Whitt, Mary Williams, Mildred Williams, Kathryn Wygal, Evelyn Berg, Rosemary Brown, Jane Day, Mildred Dodson, Cora Lee Eastwood, Aileen Farmer, Ruth Flippo, Myrtis Hall, Corinna Hammack, Mary Grace Hawkins, Katie Key, Louise Otley, Janet Patterson, Glennis Powers, Ann Rooney, Flora Ryan, Irene Lundy.

ALPHA TAU PI

NEVER before in its history has Alpha Tau Pi been so fortunate in the possession of six Seniors whose silent influence had such far-reaching effect upon campus life. Five of the six are members of the Leaders Club, of whom one was Queen of the May; and the other possessed superb talents bestowed unstintingly and unselfishly upon many a campus enterprise. When college opened, they were found backing the Y.W.C.A. and Student Council in Freshman Orientation. Early in the fall they were instrumental in starting a movement for a true honor system which is still growing on the Hill. At their instance a faculty-student conference was held in Seacobeck Dome Room, from which several movements for a true Fredericksburg spirit have grown. In the social life of the College, they were active in starting the new Cotillion Club of which most of them are members. If there is strength in union, their silent, united efforts have been crowned with the success of their labors.

Not least outstanding was the annual social occasion which this year was a stag dance given amid the classic environs of Mary Ball Dome Room, adding a touch of richness to the scene. The lovely girls stepped gaily adown the winding stairs in the figure and all who were so fortunate as to attend voted it a gala affair. The buffet service was of singular beauty, perfectly appointed, and was centered by ice punch bowls with A T II colors of red, blue, and gold shimmering through.

So ends the glory year of Alpha Tau Pi.

PI OMEGA PI

OFFICERS

DOROTHY BALLANCE . . . . . President
MISS LOLA MINICH . . . . Vice-President
MARGUERITE CRUMLEY . . . . Secretary
JESSIE CROCKETT . . . . . . Treasurer
MARGARET TWIFORD . . . . . Historian
MR. A. L. WALKER . . . . . . Sponsor

As its chief objective the Alpha Epsilon Chapter of Pi Omega Pi each year serves by contributing to the solution of some current problem in the field of education or business. It encourages high standards of ethics and scholarship in business by teaching the ideal of service as a basis of all worthy enterprise.

It is an honor to become a member of Pi Omega Pi, National Commercial Teachers honorary fraternity. Membership is gained only by those Juniors and Seniors of the commercial department who have attained superior scholastic standing in commercial subjects and at least average standing in all other subjects.

This fraternity reaches from California to Virginia and from Wisconsin to Texas. It is established only in senior teacher-training institutions and the chapter at this College is the only one in Virginia.

The highest hope of all commercial majors should be to become a member of Pi Omega Pi. It holds for them untold opportunities.

COTILLION CLUB

OFFICERS

MARGARET HAYNIE . . . . . *President*
VIRGINIA FISKE . . . . . *Vice-President*
ANN WHEAT . . . . *Secretary*
BLANCHE EDGE . . . . *Treasurer*

OF particular interest to the Freshmen was the revival this year of the Cotillion Club, as a sister organization to the German Club. With the assistance of Mrs. Frances Mooney, Miss Lillie Turman, and Miss Louise Jennings, Dr. W. J. Young reorganized the club. Later, Miss Grace Taylor was added as co-sponsor.

Anxious to begin its functions, the members met and elected officers. Under an executive committee of officers, sponsors and six members at large, the elaborate affair for their initial dance took shape.

The results of the efforts of this committee and the members became evident with its "sweetheart dance," February 12th, in which the Valentine motif was dominant. Featured in the figure, in march time, was a gigantic, lacy Valentine heart. Beneath a false ceiling of red and white cellophane and streamers shimmering in the light, the members, their escorts and other young gentlemen danced in tuneful swing-time. Never had the old gym seemed so lovely as in her Valentine dress.

With promise of climaxing this dance, the Cotillion Club has more than fulfilled the expectations of everyone. The social life of the campus is decidedly its debtor.

DRAMATIC CLUB

OFFICERS

MIRIAM CARPENTER . . . President
MARGARET CLARK . . Vice-President
JUANITA STOKES . Secretary-Treasurer

UNDER the direction of Mr. Boyce D. Loving, the new sponsor of the Dramatic Club, the first play of the season, "The Cradle Song," presented by the Dramatic Club under the sponsorship of the Y.W.C.A., demonstrated two things: that there is abundant histrionic material within the student body and that students and faculty alike will support such an effective performance as "The Cradle Song."

Between the production of "The Cradle Song" and that of "Alice-Sit-By-The-Fire," there were several shorter productions; namely, "History in Revue," five skits written by Mr. Loving, and a one-act farce, "Rich Man, Poor Man." The revue was given as a benefit for the club; the farce, a presentation at Convocation.

Differing radically in mood, setting, and story from "The Cradle Song," was "Alice-Sit-By-The-Fire," whimsical three-act comedy by Sir James M. Barrie, which was presented by the club on March 4th.

With its growth in number and talent, the Dramatic Club is considering a change in its name. Likewise, a charter will be granted the group in the national dramatic fraternity, Alpha Psi Omega. A new sponsor, improved production, possible membership in a national fraternity—all these mark the progress in affairs dramatic on the Hill.

Especial appreciation goes to Mr. Ronald Faulkner for work by the orchestra and for art work in the designing of sets, and to Mr. Harold Weiss for creating the sets. Finally, the work of the classes in Play Production was of untold value to the finished productions themselves.

MODERN PORTIAS

OFFICERS

MITCHELL FORREST LUCK . . . . President
MARGARET HAYNIE . . . . Vice-President
MILDRED POWELL . . . . Secretary
MIRIAM BOYER . . . . Treasurer
MARY GRACE HAWKINS . . . . Reporter
DR. GEORGE E. SHANKLE . . . . Sponsor

MEMBERS

Elizabeth Bodwell
Charlotte Booker
Miriam Boyer
Hazel Bricker
Dorothy Coddington
Lura Coffey
Nancy Cooper
Arcelle Coulbourn
Frances Cox
Lottie Driver
Virginia Easley
Elizabeth Evans
Hazel Ford
Ella Mae Frye

Josephine Gravett
Charlotte Hall
Ruth Harris
Mary Grace Hawkins
Margaret Haynie
Evelyn Herring
Mary T. Kettenbeck
Mitchell Forrest Luck
Virginia Meeks
Jean Moore
Nannie Moore
Gilda Oronoz
Lucille Painter
Jean Plante

Mildred Powell
Connie Reynolds
Anne Shaffer
Nancy Snead
Sally Stoakley
Clarice Taylor
Marian Timberlake
Zelma Timberlake
Ruth M. Tyler
Marcella Wells
Alyce Wenner
Evelyn Wilkinson
Elizabeth Woodbridge

MODERN PORTIAS

THE Modern Portias is the active organization of the English department
at the College, open for membership only to Juniors or Seniors having English as a major or teaching minor.

In various ways, the club encourages very generally an interest in English
classical literature. Annually it presents for the student body an interesting
and informative Convocation program. This year the program consisted of
reports on several types of writing and a lecture on a selected piece of classical literature, illustrated by colored slides.

The annual banquet was one of the most enjoyable social events of the year.
In formal attire, the members gathered about the banquet table at the Princess
Anne Hotel. After the welcoming address by the president, the club enjoyed
a delicious course dinner. The evening's entertainment was concluded by an
address on the literature of today by the sponsor of the club, Dr. George E.
Shankle.

No member of the Modern Portias can ever forget the monthly meetings of
the club which are a combination of friendly social activity and intellectual
discussion. It is the custom at this time to discuss some selected piece of
literature. At each meeting, while the members are enjoying refreshments, a
report on current events in the literary world is made.

GLEE CLUB

SWEET voices were raised in joyous song in praise to God.
It was Christmas. The Glee Club made its first formal appearance in black and white vestments. At five o'clock in the afternoon on Sunday, December 12th, they presented their annual Yuletide Concert.

Showing a great advance over any previous scope of activities, the Glee Club this year broadcast over the radio. After weeks of hard work, the Club went to Richmond, and over the local station, WRVA, offered to the radio audience a finished performance.

Following the season of the Resurrection, at Eastertide the Glee Club presented its second formal concert. The program consisted of light spring numbers and appropriate Easter music.

With the open-air theater for a setting, in June the Glee Club added their talents to the Commencement Exercises. The impressiveness of their vestments and the young voices in harmonious song added greatly to the occasion.

Members of the Glee Club spend many happy hours in creative enjoyment. They do not confine their activities to scheduled appearances. The fifty selected voices of the club take part in many formal and informal occasions throughout the entire year. To its members the club offers an intensive study of choral music and stimulates the appreciation for fine harmony.

COLLEGE ORCHESTRAS

A SUSTAINED pride, shared by all on the hill, is felt in the work of the college orchestras, which have supplied not only the charm of music with its universal appeal but these student activity groups have given gracious service, afforded hours of recreation, established purposeful objectives, and created a keener appreciation for the art. The orchestras, five in number, interest a similar number of groups—those who have had no previous experience, those who have had some training in high school orchestras, those who confine themselves to string instruments offering the type music so delightfully acceptable for teas, dinners, and receptions; the string quartet emphasizing chamber music, and last, the dance orchestra for hours in lighter vein.

Under the magic baton of the director, these orchestras have won fine recognition from the hill personnel and they have also made for an additional friendly link between the hill and the community by complying to many requests from local organizations.

LYSBETH GARTH . . . . President

THE COMMERCIAL CLUB

IN an effort to demonstrate the actual application of business skill and experience, the Commercial Club during the year made trips to several business centers. A day was spent, by three-fourths of its members, in viewing the operation of business machines in the nation's capital city. Valuable information about the function of the business woman in the world of commerce was gathered. The afternoon was spent, in lighter vein, by visiting the museums and other interesting places.

The club, later in the year, presented an enlightening convocation program. This program was in the form of a skillful demonstration of business machines by students who had completed a study of these machines.

The annual banquet of the club was held at the Stratford Hotel. Mr. Jere Willis, a distinguished citizen of Fredericksburg, was the principal speaker.

With this delightful social event, the Commercial Club climaxed a year of busy, worthwhile activity. It has been loyally supported by the students of the largest department in the College.

COMMERCIAL CLUB

SENIORS: Dorothy Ballance, Evelyn Bickers, Varina Britt, Helen Carter, Jessie Crockett, Marguerite Crumley, Edna Hersh, Betty Jones, Sue McGee, Nan Moore, Louise Otley, Robbie Pugh, Zillah Rhoades, Lily Ruff, Bertha Shapleigh, Marie Springer, Margaret Twiford, Marcella Wells.

JUNIORS: Nan Birchett, Mary Williamson Bowles, Maude Brown, Juanita Carpenter, Sarah Ann Chandler, Arcelle Coulbourne, Elizabeth Clopton, Ruth Curry, Virginia Dickinson, Margaret Emerick, Madora Forbush, Hazel Ford, Arline Garnsey, Edith Gravely, Jewell Hallett, Lucy Harris, Anne Hazlitt, Flora Lee, Pauline McConnell, Betty Louise Nolan, Maude Rae Smith, Dorothy Vernon, Georgiana Woodhouse.

SOPHOMORES: Helen Booth, Lula Bray, Phyllis Child, Helen Clark, Ruth Clark, Laura Conlon, Murlene Crush, Gladys Dutrow, Courtney Edmond, Alice Fitzhugh, Frances Green, Elizabeth Hall, Clara Harrell, Winifred Hudson, Evelyn Jones, Mabelle Knoff, Lucile Long, Eulaleur Mason, Margaret Maxwell, Eugenia Moore, Charlotte Morgan, Joanna Pappandreou, Edith Pomeroy, Kitty Roberts, Helen Dale Roop, Virginia Ramsay, Mildred Rust, Nannie Sharp, Penelope Smith, Ellen Smoot, Louise Stawls, Virginia Thomas, Nan Thompson, Cecilia Valentine, Elizabeth Weakley, Mary Lee Young.

FRESHMEN: Genevieve Allen, Janet Alston, Anne Arnold, Louellen Ashby, Charlotte Avery, Myrtle Bacon, Elizabeth Bane, Jean Becker, Martha Black, Marie Blair, Margaret Bowen, Gertrude Brandon, Virginia Bray, Dorothy Brent, Juanita Brockwell, Zane Brodie, Virginia Brothers, Emita Bruno, Nancy Burch, Helen Burrow, Marion Burroughs, Emaline Burnette, Mary Carmines, Elizabeth Carter, Kathryn Carter, Ruth Carter, Mary Carson, Marie Cattenhead, Roberta Cecil, Jane Cornwell, Eugenia Clarke, Elizabeth Cox, Carol Crafton, Dorothy Darden, Minette Dashiell, Barber Davis, Virginia Davis, Virginia Dougherty, Beryl Duell, Clara Duggan, Frances Eanes, Ruth Edwards, Eileen Emerson, Eloise Flanary, Evelyn Florence, Pauline Foster, Doris Gallant, Lucile Garrett, Ruth Garrett, Frances Gillespie, Dorothy Giles, Frances Gillum, Margaret Gillum, Virginia Gilmer, Hilda Goode, Annie Gleason, Josephine Gravett, Margaret Gregory, Mary Gunter, Martha Harrison, Helen Harwitz, Ruth Haynes, Maxine Herring, Pauline Hewitt, Lovey Hill, Nancy Hill, Marjorie Hopkins, Donald Holden, Marie Hudson, Mary Hudson, Bessie Hull, Jessie Gray Hutchinson, Bernice Ison, Jane Jennings, Geraldine Jessee, Mary Johnson, Marjorie Johnson, Aimee Jones, Dena Katz, Frances Keister, Lois Kesterson, Bertha Klann, Annie Land, Caroline Lawson, Irella Lawson, Mary Lednum, Rosa Ellen Locke, Katherine Lockhart, Ethel Loftin, Melba Loudy, Ruth MacLead, Audrey Marcy, Myra McCormick, Lida McGill, Reba McLamb, Jane Miller, Florence Moore, Miriam Morwitz, Julia Moseley, Kathryn Moss, Dorothy Munden, Jean Neate, Kathryn Newcome, Gladys Newton, Reba Nolen, Virginia Ole, Cornelia Orr, Betty Mae Owen, Constance Owens, Phyllis Pamplin, Anne Parker, Elaine Parks, Eleanor Phillips, Rosalie Radford, Charlotte Ramsburg, Virginia Reamy, Elizabeth Reed, Mary Reed, Elva Reynolds, Virginia Repass, Rosemary Rice, Mary Frances Roberts, Jean Robertson, Imogene Robinson, Frances Russell, Grace Saunders, Dorothy Seabolt, Mary Ellen Seaborne, Elizabeth Sisson, Elizabeth Smith, Dorothy Snead, Peggy Spaven, Polly Stephenson, Keta Still, Dorothy Stone, Shirley Stubbs, Dorothy Thomas, Margaret Tigner, Doris Turner, Ethel Twyford, Bernice Vellines, Ethel Ware, Janice Watson, Mary Welsh, June Wendell, Elizabeth Werth, Anne Wheat, Jean Whitley, Mary Whitt, Anne Williams, Frances Williams, Mary Williams, Sue Wohlford, Hester Wolfe, Dorothy Wood, Marjorie Wood, Marie Wright, Marguerite Wysor, Martha Yoch.

PI SIGMA KAPPA

OFFICERS

ELIZABETH TRIMBLE . . . *President*

MARY TOPP . . . . . *Vice-President*

ADELAIDE ROSBOROUGH,
                    Secretary-Treasurer

PI SIGMA KAPPA was organized early this year under the capable leadership of Dr. Almont Lindsay, assisted by Dr. Edward Alvey, Jr., Mr. Harold Weiss, and Mr. Boyce Loving. This club was formed for the purpose of encouraging interest in types of public speaking, such as informal debating, declamation, extemporaneous and after-dinner speeches.

At first membership was open to anyone, but when officers were chosen and the organization grew stronger, certain standards were set to restrict membership and the right to own the key. Greek letters were substituted for the first letters in the original name, Public Speaking Club, and the club took the name Pi Sigma Kappa.

Club members were encouraged to participate in the programs of other organizations, thereby gaining points toward their keys. The desire, on the part of the members, to own the key yielded many entertaining and informal Chapel programs.

Pi Sigma Kappa has, during the current year, sponsored the first intercollegiate debates. They have debated with teams both from Virginia colleges and also out-of-state teams.

INTERNATIONAL
RELATIONS
CLUB

"THE purpose of the Carnegie Endowment in undertaking this work of the International Relations Clubs is to instruct and to enlighten public opinion. It is not to support exclusively any one view as to how best to treat the conditions which now prevail throughout the world, but to fix the attention of students on those undying principles of international conduct, of international law, and of international organization which must be agreed upon and put into action if a peaceful civilization is to continue."

—PRESIDENT NICHOLAS MURRAY BUTLER.

The International Relations Club holds a rather unique position among the various organizations on the hill. Organized for the purpose of furthering the cause of peace, it constantly seeks, through a variety of activities, to present to the student body a message of goodwill and friendliness toward all people. The club's membership is constituted of only those students vitally interested in these challenging ideals.

THE HOME ECONOMICS CLUB

OFFICERS

VIRGINIA JORDAN . . . . President
MARGARET GIBBENS . . Vice-President
RUTH HOOKER . . . . . . Secretary
MILDRED WILLIAMS . . . Treasurer
VIRGINIA REEL . . . . . Reporter
MRS. EULA ROBINS . . . . Sponsor

A VITAL interest in the improving of meal nutrition at the Training School has been shown by the members of the Home Economics Club this year. Using the knowledge obtained from classes and meetings of the club, they have sought to improve this phase of the school life.

In its monthly meetings, the club which is affiliated with the state and national associations, has stimulated interest in its profession. The programs at these meetings have consisted of talks by outsiders and by club members, discussions of money-making projects, and plans for improving the department at the College. Of real service and pleasure to the entire student body have been the Sunday morning breakfasts and the dinners served to various organizations.

By helping as hostesses in entertaining the Virginia State Legislature, the club feels that it, undoubtedly, broadened its associations and professional opportunities.

OFFICERS

Marie Springer . . . . . . President
Dorothy Miller . . . Vice-President
Louise Godwin . . . . . . Secretary
Margaret Gibbens . . . . Treasurer
Betty Garden,
    Chairman of Social Committee
Calvert Spillman,
    Chairman of Program Committee
Helen Hill,
    Chairman of Initiation Committee
Henrietta Roberts . . . . Reporter

MATHEW FONTAINE MAURY
SCIENCE CLUB

THIS year the Science Club has endeavored to develop and expand the members' interest in the various fields of science. Individual participation in its round-table discussions was encouraged by a choice of subjects closely connected with the personal interests of the members. One of the most delightful and heated discussions was on the subject of cosmetics. At another of its informal meetings the club was entertained by the Freshman science class of the College Training School.

Dr. Roy S. Cook
Sponsor

THE RIDING CLUB

OFFICERS

EULALIA BOWLING . . . . *President*

MAUDE RAE SMITH . . . . . . *Vice-President*

MARGARET WALLACE . . . *Secretary-Treasurer*

WITH the arrival of spring on the hill, jodhpurs, boots, and riding crops are given most publicity. The annual horseshow of the Riding Club is awaited with great anticipation.

In the horse show the members of the club compete with those of equal ability. There are prizes and trophies for winners in the various events. Cups are awarded to those who excel in special events. A most attractive feature is the costume class. Great skill is shown in the jumping events. But most coveted of all awards

is the College Cup, which is given to the most
outstanding rider in the show.

Throughout the year, the club has enjoyed
picnics in rustic settings at the end of rides
through the surrounding country. Through
wood and brush, over hills and streams, they
ride in good fellowship. Sometimes these rides
end with basket suppers. Favorite of all rides
are those made by moonlight.

Forgetting the bridle path for an afternoon,
the Riding Club set a precedent socially this
fall. They gave one of the most enjoyable social
events of the year in the form of a tea in the
spacious Dome Room of Seacobeck Hall.

The German Club

Officers

Alice Rife, President   Mary Jack Clary, Secretary   Miriam Carpenter, Treasurer

Roster

Peggy Austin
Martha Lee Bennett
Charlotte Booker
Eulalia Bowling
Frances Brooks
Eloise Caverlee
Margaret Clark
Dorothy Coddington
Nancy Cooper
Mary Lawrence Davenport
Elsie Lee Davis
Georgia Lou Easterling
Marjorie Eastman
Jo Lee Fleet
Jane Haddox
Edna Hersh

Roster

Rosalie Johnson
Virginia Jordon
Ethel Hartman
Stirling Kerr
Margaret McCulloch
Mary Franklin Miller
Mary Lou Monroe
Doris O'Brien
Jean Plante
Jean Robertson
Connie Rollins
Mildred Rawls
Catherine Rucker
Eleanor Small
Juanita Stokes
Elizabeth Trimble

Sponsor

Mrs. Charles Lake Bushnell

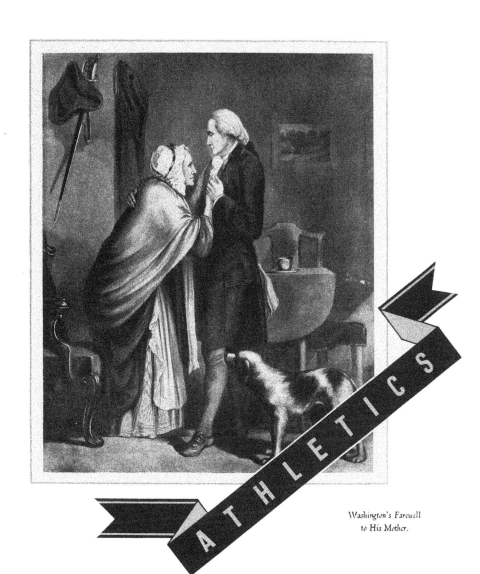

ATHLETICS

Washington's Farewell
to His Mother.

IN an effort to interest every student on the hill and all outsiders, the Athletic Association, led by a council comprised of
the chairmen of such seasonal sports as hockey, basketball, swimming, and baseball, this year spread its activities beyond the usual
intramural competition.

In the fall, in addition to the beginning competition for the
Devil-Goat Cup, the A.A. sent representatives to the Virginia
Field Hockey Tournament at Harrisonburg. The experience
gleaned at this meet will undoubtedly pay large dividends.

No greater progress in any field of athletics has been made
than by the newly formed Swimming Club. Of particular interest
was their participation in the National Telegraphic Swimming
Meet. Safer and more instructive plunge hours are now assured.
This has been made possible by the assumption on the part of the
Senior Red Cross Life-Savers of full charge of the plunge hours.

The Freshmen this year defeated the Sophomores at basketball!
Until that time the latter team had been undefeated. This was
only one surprise of a fast-moving season, which culminated in the
tournament at Williamsburg.

No student can ever forget the accomplishments of the Athletic
Association this year. Future Associations would do well to
aspire to meet and surpass it.

A Champion Volley.

Left-hand lunge and the ball is hers.

Court 'n' a goal.

Tee for two.

"Come on in; the water's fine."

A motif in black and white.

Court 'n' a goal.

Tee for two.

"Come on in; the water's fine."

A motif in black and white.

[151]

Personality in living statuary.

DANCE CLUB

OFFICERS

DELLA RICKS . . . . . . President
EDNA HERSH . . . . Vice-President
LEONORA WEISS . . . . . Secretary

CAPTURE the spirit of movement. Then combine this with the spirit of music. This has been the new program of the Modern Dance Club for 1937-38. Once a week they have met in fitting attire to combine a study of technique with inspiration.

Out of this new plan of rendition, the Modern Dance Club presented a beautiful program in the open-air theater. In midwinter the club attended the annual Symposium of Modern Dance sponsored by George Washington University in Washington, D.C. Here they exchanged theories with dance groups representing girls' colleges in Virginia, Maryland, and the District of Columbia..

In early spring the club presented a program of Modern Dance at the meeting of the Physical Education Association of Virginia, which was held at Washington and Lee University in Lexington, Virginia.

Each year the Dance Club plays a prominent part in the May Day exercises. Much of the theme and story of this annual program is interpreted by the dance.

FEATURES

The Tomb of Mary Washington—a
tribute in marble from the Women of
America to the Woman of America.

LOUISE JEANNETTE OTLEY
Authority without ostentation; leniency when merited.

[156]

JANE EMILIE SINCLAIR

A smooth, easy efficiency, always sufficient unto the day.

[157]

HELEN WADE PRESSLEY

A joyous disposition combined with a purposeful earnestness.

[158]

FLORA RUBY RYAN

Sustained enthusiasm and unselfishness that is not strained.

[159]

ELIZABETH McCLINTIC TRIMBLE

Winsome manner and unruffled mien, but analytical of mind and persevering in purpose.

[160]

CLARICE TAYLOR

Much fine metal here—a golden voice and a heart of gold and sterling worth always.

[161]

Picking was good.

Forgotten.

That Long, White Line.

FRANCES GRAY NASH
Winner of the Kiwanis Cup, 1937
Recognition justly bestowed for services rendered.

Just Kidding.

Will Be Children.

Kerchiefs, kerchiefs everywhere
And not one unbecoming.

She keeps faith with the stars and stripes.

October 31—In the mood and in the mode with Goblins on parade.

MIRIAM CARPENTER

Princess to the 1938 Apple Blossom Festival, Winchester, Virginia.

The Gathering of the Nuts.

Sweethearts on Parade.

Senior Day, when "larnin'" is
minimized and comradeship is king.

The Shamrock had its night.

March 26—The Class of '37 acts up
melodramatically.

The struggle stupendous by the two-legged Goats.

Jeanne meets Jean.
Devil meets Goat.
Victor meets Vanquished.

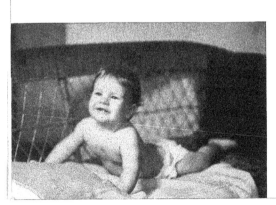

Charles George Gordon Moss, Junior.
Already on the official College calling list.

A Devilish Group.

Virginia Hall—Survival of the fittest
in the Intra-Dormitory Games.

MARGARET HAYNIE

Queen of the May

VIRGINIA ANDERSON
Maid of Honor

MAY COURT

The Spring of Nineteen Nundred and Thirty-eight

MAY QUEEN
MARGARET HAYNIE

MAID OF HONOR
VIRGINIA ANDERSON

MAIDS

EULALIA BOWLING	VIRGINIA JORDAN
FRANCES BROOKS	MARY ELLEN LEE
MIRIAM CARPENTER	MARGARET McCULLOCH
MARY JACK CLARY	NANCY MOSELEY
NANCY COOPER	MARGARET CLARK
ELSIE LEE CORNWELL	BEULAH MASON
VIRGINIA FISKE	GLENNIS POWERS
JO LEE FLEET	ALICE RIFE
MADORA FORBUSH	BEVERLY ROBERTS
CHARLOTTE GOURLEY	MAY LAWRENCE SHOWARD
CORNELIA IRBY	MAUDE RAE SMITH
JEANNE JOHNSON	ELIZABETH WOODHOUSE

HERALDS

FRANCES GILLUM	MARGARET GILLUM

FLOWER GIRLS

HELEN CLARK	CATHERINE MOSS

TRAIN BEARERS

POLLY STEPHENSON	MARTHA RAMSEY

CROWN BEARER
MASTER TOM KING, JR.

SENIOR ROSTER

Evelyn Andrews . . . . . 206 Dillard Street,
Martinsville, Virginia

Dorothy Ballance . . . . . Hickory, Virginia

Evelyn Bickers . . . . . . 601 Blue Ridge Avenue,
Culpeper, Virginia

Irene Blasdel . . . . Box 15, Swarthmore, Pennsylvania

Varina Britt . . . . 702 High Street,
Franklin, Virginia

Helen Ford Carter . . . . Gate City, Virginia

Mary Jack Clary . . . . . Bowling Green, Virginia

Lura Finley Coffey . . . . 704 Memorial Avenue,
North Wilkesboro, North Carolina

Nancy Cooper . . . . . . Niles, Michigan, R.F.D. No. 1

Frances Cox . . . . 2453 Wisconsin Avenue, N.W.,
Washington, D.C.

Jessie Marie Crockett . . . 350 LaSalle Avenue,
Hampton, Virginia

Marguerite Crumley . . . . 1017 Euclid Avenue,
Bristol, Virginia

Mary Lawrence Davenport . Pitt Street,
Pactolus, North Carolina

Virginia Jane Davis . . . . 832 West Beverley Street,
Staunton, Virginia

Gladys Dickerson . . . . . 903 West Street, Laurel, Delaware

Virginia Easley . . . . . . Chatham, Virginia, R.F.D. No. 2

Margaret Louise Gibbens . . 447 North Loudoin Street,
Winchester, Virginia

Louise Godwin . . . . . . Windsor, Virginia

Frances Jo Grant . . . . . Culpeper, Virginia

Anna Mae Harris . . . . . Lignum, Virginia

Mary Grace Hawkins . . . 132 Archer Avenue,
Petersburg, Virginia

Margaret Haynie . . . . . Irvington, Virginia

Edna M. Hersh . . . . . . Balboa Heights, Canal Zone

Helen G. Hill . . . . . . Box 313, Appalachia, Virginia

Cornelia Irby . . . . Blackstone, Virginia

Elizabeth Jones . . . . . . New Castle, Virginia

Virginia Jordan . . . . . . 6152 Rolfe Avenue,
Norfolk, Virginia

Stirling Kerr . . . . Arlington, Virginia

Mary T. Kettenbeck . . . . Farmington, Connecticut

Doris Lafoon . . . . Alberta, Virginia

Mary Ellen Lee . . . . . . 18 Ewan Terrace,
Vineland, New Jersey

Mitchell Forrest Luck . . . 818 Wolfe Street,
Fredericksburg, Virginia

Irene Lundy . . . . Emporia, Virginia

Martha Sue McGee . . . . Lawrenceville, Georgia

Virginia Moore Meeks . . . 225 Western Avenue,
Rocky Mount, North Carolina

Dorothy Miller . . . . . . 1410 Allene Avenue, S.W.,
Atlanta, Georgia

Mary Franklyn Miller . . . 4534 Burlington Place, N.W
Washington, D.C.

Jean Moore . . . . Norton, Virginia

Nannie Moore . . . . . . Odd, Virginia

Annie Mae Morris . . . . . Beaver Dam, Virginia

Louise Otley . . . . Purcellville, Virginia

Lucy Payne . . . . Warrenton, Virginia

Katherine Pearman . . . . 34 Fillmore Street,
Petersburg, Virginia

Jean Plante . . . . 81 Electric Street,
Worcester, Massachusetts

Helen Pressley . . . . . . Elkridge, Maryland

Mary Robert Pugh . . . . 1457 Berkeley Avenue
Petersburg, Virginia

Miriam Puster . . . . . . North Emporia, Virginia

Corinne Reynolds . . . . . Chatham, Virginia

Zillah Rhoades . . . . . . Culpeper, Virginia

Della Ricks . . . . Blacksburg, Virginia

Alice Rife . . . . Smithfield, Virginia

Mary Lily Ruff . . . . . . Bedford, Virginia

Flora R. Ryan . . . . . . 8 Irving Place,
Nutley, New Jersey

Grace Schultz . . . . . . Citronelle, Alabama

Bertha M. Shapleigh . . . . Eastham, Virginia

May Lawrence Showard . . Chincoteague Island, Virginia

Elsie Marie Smith . . . . . Buckner, Virginia

Isabel Smith . . . . Threeway, Virginia

Nancy Snead . . . . 144 Carroll Avenue,
Petersburg, Virginia

Lucille Snellings . . . . . 800 Mercer Street,
Fredericksburg, Virginia

Calvert Spillman . . . . . Index, Virginia

Marie E. Springer . . . . . 4220 Omohundro Street,
Norfolk, Virginia

Clarice Taylor . . . . . . 210 Hawthorne Street,
Colonial Beach, Virginia

Zelma Timberlake . . . . . Sweet Hall, Virginia

Walteen Tolley . . . . . . Crimora, Virginia, R.F.D. No. 1

Elizabeth McClintic Trimble . Hot Springs, Virginia

Margaret Twiford . . . . . Wardtown, Virginia

Ida Lee Twiss . . . . . . Edgartown, Virginia

Marcella Wells . . . . . . Carson, Virginia, R.F.D. No. 1

Elizabeth W. Woodbridge . 605 Hauke Street,
Fredericksburg, Virginia

Compliments
of

THE SOUTHERN GRILL

**The Most Modern Restaurant in
Fredericksburg, Virginia**

PRIVATE BANQUET ROOM

Winter and Summer — Air Conditioned

Where the

Romance of the Old

Meets the Progress of

the New

ༀ

**CITY OF
FREDERICKSBURG**

THE
STRATFORD HOTEL

Fireproof

**Fredericksburg's Newest and
Finest Hotel**

On Highway Route 1

E. G. HEFLIN
Owner-Director

Compliments

of

A Friend

Judson Smith

MAIN STREET

FREDERICKSBURG, VIRGINIA

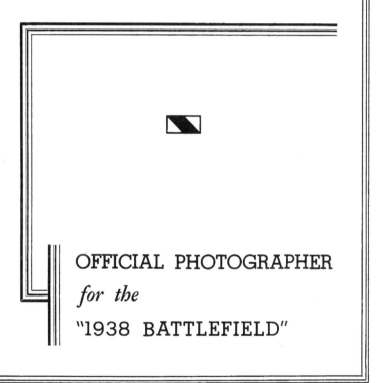

OFFICIAL PHOTOGRAPHER
for the
"1938 BATTLEFIELD"

Member of

The College Annual Producers of the United States

THOMSEN-ELLIS CO.

COLLEGE ANNUALS
VIEW BOOKS · CATALOGS
ADVERTISING LITERATURE

BALTIMORE
NEW YORK

Printers of the 1938 BATTLEFIELD